Person-Centred Planning Course Book

OTHER PUBLICATIONS IN THE SERIES:

For information on this or other courses please contact:

LEARN CARE EXCEL

Matthews House
21 Thorley Park Road
Bishops Stortford
CM23 3NG

Tel: 07774 880880
info@learncareexcel.co.uk
www.learncareexcel.co.uk

Contents

INTRODUCTION

Too frequently in the past people at the centre of a care concern found themselves in a position where they felt that the care was being done "to" them rather than "for" them, leaving them feeling as though they had very little say in their life. All too often the plan of about what should happen was decided by how much something would cost or what fit into the schedule. The trouble was, this meant that the basic wishes of the person at the centre were often overlooked. There may even have been times when, if they'd have been listened to, there would have been no conflict between what the person wanted and what worked well for the whole team. And sometimes, paying attention to and carrying out the person's wishes might even have produced a more desirable outcome.

This is why PERSON-CENTRED PLANNING (PCP) has become the standard approach to the care of vulnerable individual, such as the elderly, those with learning difficulties or physical disabilities, and those with dementia or mental health issues. It allows people to have control over their own lives, making their own decisions about how they wish to live.

According to the CQC and the National Minimum Standards, everyone in care must have a care plan detailing their daily requirements physical, medical and personal requirements but a PCP goes into much more detail about the individual right down to how they have their tea and what time they like to go to bed.

Initially this may seem a lot more work than old models of care but, with a little more effort in the beginning the person at the centre of the care will feel more listened to and valued and will be more content about the way they are treated, making them less likely to "buck the system" later meaning that things will run more smoothly in the long run. It is for this reason that a PCP is currently being seen as the best option for planning care while still respecting the individual at its centre and should be enthusiastically embraced by care providers.

As with all the texts in this series, information in this course book is aimed at workers in the care industry and discussion will concentrate particularly on the care and treatment of adults in these settings. If you are supporting younger people or those with special needs please consult further texts.

HISTORY AND ORIGINS

For many years there had been a belief that care institutions were failing those they had been set up to support by not treating them as individuals and, hence, devaluing and dehumanising them. They were denied the chance at a "normal" life and treated more as an "inmate" than a person in need of assistance. In 1969 Wolf Wolfensberger, in his Normalisation Theory, even went so far as to say they were treated as "abnormal" once they were in these institutions because they were away from the "valued, normal" lifestyles of family, work and friendships.

John O'Brien's work followed on from this initial theory and he developed a set of valued human experiences along with a framework for service providers (care providers) to help individuals in achieving these "valued" lifestyles called the "Five Essential Service Accomplishments".

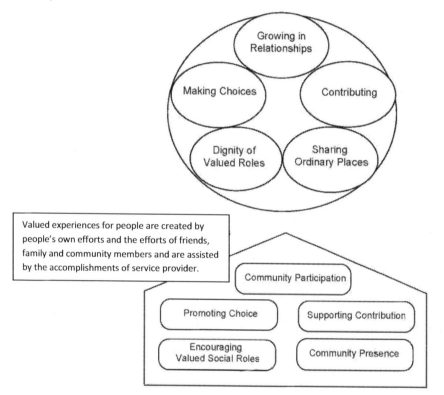

This diagram shows the significant part played by community participation

Today, community participation developed into community inclusion and means that in order to get the most out of their lives someone must be an active participant in the decisions surrounding that life as well as the lives of those around them. Equally, community inclusion means that it is not enough to simply 'take part' in the community but that the community embraces **all** of its members, including the people with support needs.

In his continuing work O'Brien worked in conjunction with others to develop the "**ALL MEANS ALL**"[1] list expressing the parameters and values of inclusion to go along with his Essential Services model:

> All people have a right to live in and be part of the community
>
> All people have a voice and a right to be heard
>
> All people have a right to dreams and aspirations
>
> All people have capabilities and qualities
>
> All people should have the opportunity to live an ordinary and valued life
>
> All people should have power and control over what they do now and in the future
>
> All people need friendships and independent relationships; a natural support network
>
> The whole community can benefit from embracing diversity

The medical role of disability *versus* the social role of disability

These developments all led to a change in the approach to the care of people who need extra support. Previously someone who needed extra help had to conform to societies preconceived ideas of their position and abilities within that society. If they were disabled or had learning difficulties or were old and frail, their bodies (symptoms, conditions) were treated but their emotional well-being (hopes, desires, likes, life learning and individuality) was ignored. People were institutionalised with the assumption that they were there to be "cured" and would remain in the institution until they could conform to what was seen as "normal" in society at that time. This is called the **'medical model'**.

Today the **'social model'** of care has made the medical model outdated as it recognises that people are individuals who have a valuable contribution to make to society, regardless of their need for extra help. "People are disabled by society's attitude towards them". The social model focuses upon the person not the impairment and asks how society can support the person in taking their full role.

The medical model would hold a person back until they proved they are "ready" to move on. The problem with this approach was that, all too often, the level of expectation was set too high meaning that individual had too mammoth a task to achieve before they were "ready" and may never be "ready" at all. The social model, however seeks to find ways that society can be adapted so that it is not the person who must be ready for society but society who is made ready for them.

---

[1] Source: C-change.org.uk

There has been extensive research into the field of providing a respectful, inclusive life for those in need of care support and in addition to **Wolf Wolfensberger** and **John O'Brien** other people such as **Helen Sanderson, Peter Kinsella, Simon Duffy, Michael W Smull** and **Connie Lyle O'Brien** have all made significant advancements which have led to the development and adoption of the Person-Centre Plan. The internet is a great resource for finding out more about these people and their work and some of them are referred to later in this book as well as a full list of their accomplishments at the end.

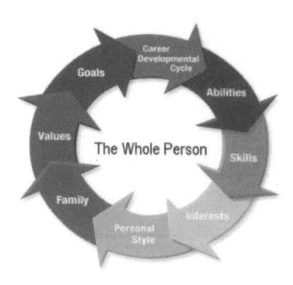

VALUES OF A PERSON-CENTRED APPROACH

One of the core features of a PCP is allowing the service user to make their own decisions even if they lead to mistakes. Below are some comments from people with learning disabilities in this regard[2]:

- "Trust in me to have a go even if I fail"
- "I want good explanations as to why I'm not to do things"
- "I want to be able to go out on my own."
- "I want a chance to do things for myself like make my own hot drinks or cook a meal."
- "I want to develop; move forward not backward"
- What risky things do you do now? "Nothing – everything gets done for me at home."
- "I used to make myself hot drinks but now I don't have the confidence to do that."
- "People are scared because things in my life went wrong so they try to protect me too much."

These quotes express some of the very simple desires and wishes people may have. Not being able to do them can make them feel less respected, less valued, less human. The values at the centre of PCP planning seek to restore the sense of "humanness" that a person may have lost, often through nothing more than just growing old. Values that a PCP restores to a person include:

Individuality	Independence	Privacy
Dignity	Respect	Choice
Rights	Responsibilities	Citizenship
Inclusion		Partnership

In order to truly achieve these a carer needs a certain set of skills:

Empathy	Listening skills
Patience	Good communication skills
Respect for others	Determination
Trust	

Please note that, although people involved in a caring for someone will need to have all of these skills to an extent, as the relationship with the service user differs (for instance care home manager as opposed to a day carer) so too does the emphasis on certain of the skills above.

---

[2] Source: www.cumbria.gov.uk/elibrary/Content/Internet/327/877/1078/39162131814.pdf

FOCUSING ON THE POSITIVES

Following on from the discussions in the previous section about respect, inclusivity and concentrating on what people are able to do (rather than what they are not) the key component in any PCP is positivity. From the point of view of a care provider in a nursing home this means identifying the ways in which the home itself inhibits a person from doing what they would like, rather than assuming it is the person's own incapacities that are the barrier. Focus must be on what they can do rather than what they cannot; on how they might succeed at their goals rather than the ways they could fail.

In their book "People, Plans and Possibilities – exploring Person-Centred Planning" (1997), Sanderson et al gave the description of PCP as follows:

"[Not simply] just the latest way of doing individual programme plans or assessments, [but] a set of beliefs and values."

In 'A little book on Person-Centred Planning' edited by John O'Brien and Connie Lyle O'Brien they state that:

"Person-Centred Planning begins when people decide to listen carefully and in ways that can strengthen the voice of people who have been or are at risk of being silenced. [It] celebrates, relies on, and finds its sober hope in people's interdependence."

However successful PCPs can only be achieved if managers are prepared to give away power, take risks and commit to providing resources to the people in their charge. A bureaucratic approach can hinder the open mindedness and vision that is required to truly achieve success for all the people involved. PCP is not itself an assessment, but rather an approach to the way assessments are carried out where the very first thought is "what **can** be done?"

Remember: It is the person who leads the care plan not the other way around

PUTTING IT INTO PRACTICE

Often identifying and communicating our likes, dislikes, choice, hopes and dreams is not the problem. We can let people know how we have our coffee or that we like to read the papers with dinner or that we are looking forward to seeing our grandchild's graduation ceremony.

So why should it be so different if we find ourselves in need of support for certain parts of our life. Just because independence in some areas of our life is now hindered does not mean that we relinquish our right to it altogether. It is probably more important, at times when we need extra help, that we do not undervalue our choices and preferences and spend a bit of extra effort ensuring that they are communicated well to those who now assist us. Otherwise, how can we expect anything other than receiving what **they** thought we need and want? This can be very frustrating for both parties as the one not getting what they want can become agitated and the one trying to help can feel confused.

When we rely on others for support we need to let them know about every preference we have (if any), right down to what order we like to put our clothes on. This is when a PCP can give back a person some control over their lives.

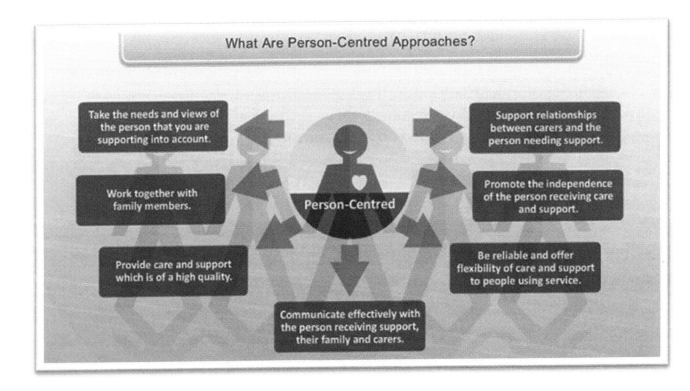

Ironically the best person to carry out a PCP is the person for whom it is being done, so that they can feel in control of the process. Having the choice of who attends any meetings, where and when they should be held and what action should be taken empowers and engages the looked after person right from the beginning. They are the ones who are best able to identify their future goals and ask for the support that is needed.

In reality, the majority of people with a PCP are unable to do all of this on their own as they would probably not require the PCP if they were able. There may issues around communication, cognitive deficits, physical and emotional limitations or even just a lack of computer skills. Others may lack confidence, be afraid of change or simply be conditioned to the fact that other people have always made decisions for them.

There is nothing to stop friends and family putting PCP into practice on behalf of a loved one. In fact, families should be encouraged to work together to plan for what the looked after person may need or want in the future. The input of friends and family will not be compromised by the financial pressures and time constraints in the way that a care home Manager's would be. In fact, recently more and more training on putting together a PCP is being offered to self-advocates, parents and friends and grown-up children as well as care staff.

Additionally, it is fair to say that traditionally there has been a rift between the opinions of professional, qualified personnel, and the loved ones of service users. This is the perfect example of how 'power' and perceived 'best interests' can hamper the progress of the service user. The strength of PCP is derived from co-operation, sharing and communication, not from competition, power struggles and distrust.

The person is the expert on the subject of themselves, not the professional.

CIRCLE OF SUPPORT

Sometimes known as a "Circle of Friends" this refers to a group of people who know and care about an individual and use their knowledge of that person to bring their skills, networks and efforts in to look after the person. Often this is just the friends and family who a have developed an informal but effective support system for the person.

Ideally, the service user can choose who they invite into their circle so that they know and trust them. However, this is not always possible due to the limited networks available to the service user or the difficulty they have maintaining relationships due to time, location or even technological restrictions.

The alternative is either to have no circle at all or to compromise by involving the people who are around and care for the person, even though they are paid staff. The trouble with having paid staff within the circle of support is sometimes they may be conflicted when it comes to speaking out for the service user due to pressures from management, time constraints, organisational policies or funding restrictions. The aim is to assemble a group of people to focus on the service user as an equal to support them in achieving their individual goals in the long term. Paid staff may not be in a position to offer this continuity.

"A circle of friends is something that many of us take for granted unless we do not have one.
A circle of friends provides us with a network of support of family and friends.
A circle of friends is available when loving advice or physical support is needed"[3]

_____

[3] Source: Perske & Perske cited in Teaching English Learners in Inclusive Classrooms (2006) E. Duran

BARRIERS TO PCP

While the benefits of a PCP are accepted it is recognised that PCP is not the simplest nor the easiest approach to setting up a plan to look after someone in care. Here are just some of the factors that can make a PCP difficult.

- **Funding:** a service user may have very little money (or their money may be tied up) and sorting out exactly what they have or are entitled to, and how to get access to it can be incredibly complicated and often can take time and negotiating. There must also be consideration given to their existing expenses before spending it elsewhere.

- **Buildings:** practical restrictions, such as health and safety requirements, or issues with the layout of the building in which the services user lives may exist.

- **Staff rotas:** staff may not be available when a service user wishes for many reasons such as outside commitments or illness.

- **Policies and procedures** – these can be restrictive to the service user, and though they may wish to help, ultimately staff must comply with the regulations in order to keep their job.

- **Documentation:** a PCP can be very paper-work intensive committing people to complete forms, come up with individual plans and review them periodically.

- **PCP itself could be confused with the actual goal:** sometimes the person preparing the PCP can become so invested in the plan itself that they see it as the ultimate goal and forget that the goal is to provide the service user with a way to fulfil their needs and desires.

- **Segregated services:** as service users become involved with various institutions there can be additional PCPs drawn up which may have mismatches. Parts of the PCP may end up being missed off while others are duplicated.

- **Lack of motivation:** if a PCP is to be successful it must go at the service users own pace which staff may wish could be quicker than the actual pace. This may result in demotivation or distraction.

- **Lack of leadership:** without good leadership a PCP can lose direction or suffer from a lack of engagement.

A PERSON-CENTRED APPROACH TO RISK

"Risk can become a highly charged and politically loaded issue. The parties involved can have very different interests at stake ..., leading to different parties taking entrenched positions that prevent cooperation, agreement and action and further trap the person." [4]

Finding a way to promote rights without failing in the duty of care is the challenge.

Services are often good at highlighting the downsides of a proposal but can be poor at thinking about the benefits. There are great opportunities in facing up to risk and finding positive solutions.

A POSITIVE APPROACH TO RISK REQUIRES PERSON-CENTRED THINKING!

PERSON-CENTRED THINKING REQUIRED A POSITIVE APPROACH TO RISK! [5]

Traditional methods of risk assessment are full of charts and scoring systems, but the person, their objectives, dreams and life seem to get lost somewhere in the pages of tick boxes and statistics. PCP recognises the importance of people's rights, including the right to make 'bad' decisions. Keeping the person at the "centre" and gathering the fullest information possible to demonstrate that all the issues have been given due consideration, allows people to make decisions together, based on what is important to the person, what is needed to keep them healthy and safe, and what will maintain a positive impact on the community.

The government says "It should be possible for a person to have a support plan which enables them to manage identified risks and to live their lives in ways which best suit them"[6]. In order to achieve this, a PCP approach is required, to help people, and those who care about them, think in a positive and productive way about how to ensure that they can achieve the things they want to see while keeping risk in its place.

In his book The Risk Management of Everything: Rethinking the Politics of Uncertainty[7], Michael Power calls for "intelligent" risk management that does not "swamp managerial attention and independent critical imagination" and suggest that the best way to achieve this is by "learning and experiment rather than rule based processes" and which stand up to challenge, questioning and criticism. The Better Regulation Commission has called for the emphasis in risk management to shift toward "resilience, self-reliance, freedom, innovation and a spirit of adventure".

---

[4] Source: A Positive Approach To Risk Requires Person Centred Thinking (2008) Neill et al
[5] Source: The Right to Take Risks: Service Users' Views of Risk in Adult Care - jrf.org.uk
[6] Source: Department of Health 2007
[7] Source: The Risk Management of Everything: Rethinking the Politics of Uncertainty (2004) M. Power

BATES AND SILBERMAN'S CRITERIA

The experience of many people who have to rely on care providers for their support is that "risk" is the reason they are given as to why they cannot do the things that other people are doing every day. Unfortunately, in modern society the unpredictable actions of an individual can have an amplified impact on the reputation of services, and on political and corporate institutions. As we progress into a society dominated by the fear of "risk" concerns such as "reputational risk management" and the fear of being sued govern many of our decisions.

In the case of human services, this means an ever more intrusive and obsessive focus on every aspect of the lives, behaviours and even potential behaviours of the people they support. It can also mean an increase "proceduralisation" of work as defensive mechanism. "Blame avoidance" becomes more important than the lives of individual people at the centre of care.

Bates and Silberman have described effective risk management as the "holy grail" of mental health and other care services. It recognises that life and risk are inseparable and look at risk from the point of view of the person, their family and friends and the wider community, rather than solely from the point of view of the service provider. They argue that any such approach would need to meet a number of requirements.[8]

- Involvement of Service Users and relatives in risk assessment
- Positive and Informed risk taking
- Proportionality (weighing up the risk of harm against the actual harm that might be caused, along with the practicality of eliminating that risk)
- Contextualising behaviour (looking at the activity within its setting and not in isolation)
- Defensible decision making (having sensible reasons to back up a decision)
- A learning culture
- Tolerable risk (accepting a risk if it is not too great and furthers the goals of the individual)

They see effective risk taking as finding a balance between "positive risk taking" involving the values independence while minimising the risk of harm to the person and the community.

---

[8] Source: A Positive Approach To Risk Requires Person Centred Thinking (2008) Neill et al

A Person Centred Approach To Risk

Purpose   People   Process   Progress

1. Who is the person
- What people like and admire about the person, what is important to them and how best to support them.

2. Where are we now?
- What is working and not working from the person's perspective and others perspectives?
- Clarify the risk – what is the problem you are trying to solve?

3. Where do we want to be?
- What does success looks like, for the person and others.

4. What have we tried and learned already?
- What have you tried and learned already?
- What are the consequences if we do nothing?

5. What shall we do next?
- What is obvious?
- What are potential solutions?
- How do the potential solutions measure up to what matters to the person?
- What will you try? Who will do what, by when?
- How can you ensure that the person has as much choice and control in this as possible?
- What are your responsibilities?
- What does good support means in implementing the action plan?
- How will you record what you are learning?
- What can you do if things don't go to plan?

9

---

[9] Source: By Bob Wade of Care To Train Ltd

There are a number of styles and techniques that have been developed for service staff to use when preparing a PCP. The terminology and style of each one may differ slightly but the fundamental principles of independence, choice, inclusion, equality and empowerment remain throughout. It is the job of the service provider to identify which method is best suited to each individual.

Good Day / Bad Day Tool

One of the easiest and best tools is the "Good Day / Bad Day" [10]tool:

- A good day is a day that the person enjoys, finds meaningful, feels they have achieved something or connected with other people. It is a day where much of what is important to the person is present, and where they have stayed healthy and safe in a way that makes sense to them.

- A bad day is a day that the person does not enjoy or find meaningful, where they feel nothing has been achieved, where what is important to them has mainly not been present and where they have not been healthy or safe, or where they have been kept healthy and safe in a way that does not make sense for them.

The Process:
1. Think together with the person and the people who know and care most about them:

   - What makes a good day for the person?
   - Who is usually there on good days?
   - What kinds of things does the person do?
   - What places does the person go?
   - Are there any important objects or routines that help make a good day?

2. Think about the same questions for a bad day.

3. Make a picture or description together of what makes a really good day and what makes a really bad day.

4. Make a plan together about ways to have more good days and fewer bad days and write this down. **Make sure you know WHO will do WHAT and by WHEN.**

---

[10] Source: www.elpnet.net

5. It is also possible to develop a tables which can be used at the beginning of the process but will also serve the monitor progress.

Communication Chart

When this is happening (or has just happened)?	How is it done?	What do we think it means?	What should be done?
The context, the environment, the event or trigger	The behaviour, what others notice, what can be seen, heard and felt by others	The feelings and emotions about it	What the person wants others to do or not do

Staff Matching Chart

Supports - wanted and needed	Skills needed
Personality characteristics	Shared common interests

Learning Logs

Date	Who was there	What happened	What went well? What did you learn?	What did not go well? What did you learn?

Another method of developing a PCP is the 4 +1 Questions by Michael Smull

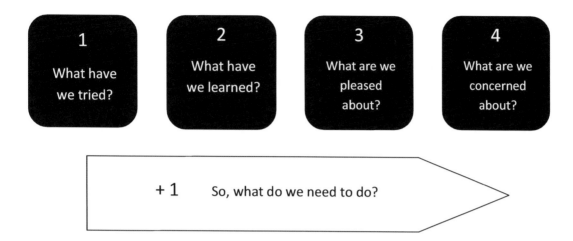

The 4+1 questions are a useful way that a person and the people who care about them most can think together about important issues. If the questions are used properly, everyone will get a chance to share their experiences and voice their concerns.

Sometimes the questions can be used to review what has happened since the last meeting. Sometimes they can be used to look at a specific issue that needs more in depth thought.

Ideas Evaluation Tool

Alternatively the Ideas Evaluation Tool developed by John O'Brien can be of use.

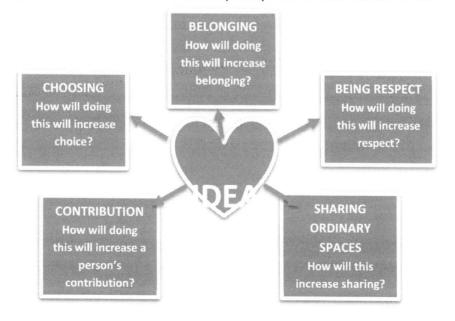

Communication Passport

This passport, developed by Max Neil in 2006, is to be completed with the person and the people who know them best and spend most time with them. These people are the experts on how the person communicates.

People who know the person well should:

- Think about the questions on the form
- Spend time with the person, listening to them with their ears, eyes, minds and hearts
- Meet together with the person to think about how that person communicates, one question at a time
- Be honest and realistic

The more time spent thinking and talking about the questions, the better the answers will be. The format of the passport can be adapted to suit the person.

Communication passport Everyone has their own special ways of communicating how they feel, what they like and dislike, what they want and don't want. Writing down the ways that gets the message across will help more people understand what is being said.	What does the person like?	How do we know?

How does the person respond to...	Response/behaviour
The spoken word	
Sights	
Sounds	
Touch	
Smell	
Atmospheres	

In this situation	When the person does this	We think it means this	And we do this

We want to tell this person	To do this …	Helped/supported by

What are the best times and places to communicate with the person?	Who are the people who are best at communicating with them? Why?

What is the best way to communicate with the person?

The passport is never finished. As more things are learned about how the person communicates and as the person's communication changes, things can be changed and added to the form.

The Lifeline Tool (sometimes also called a 'history map'.)

Gather together people who know and care about the person, especially those who have known the person for a long time. Collect any other information you have about the person's history; old records, photographs, precious objects, and anything else that helps.

Use the lifeline to picture the person's life, from when they were born to the present day. Record important people in the person's life, places they have been significant events, achievements and turning points.

Use words and pictures and anything that works for the person. Make the lifeline as big as it needs to be to include everything that shows how the person has got to where they are today. If there are big gaps, think about how you will find out how to fill them.

Thinking about the past can bring back bad memories as well as good ones. Be ready to support the person and their friends and family if they feel upset about some of the events from their past.

Sometimes this can be followed by using the dreams tool to think about the person's dreams for the future and possibly the nightmares that they definitely do not want in their future, or by thinking about what the person's gifts and skills are and ways they can use these gifts to make a contribution to the community and connect with others.

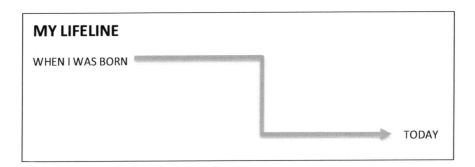

Essential Lifestyle Planning (ELP)[11]

Essential lifestyle planning began in the late 1980's at the University of Maryland and is fundamentally, the plan is developed by spending time and listening to the person and others who know and care about them:

- Finding out what is important to someone
- Learning about what health, safety and risk means to the individual and those who know and care about him or her
- Figuring out how someone can be supported in having a balance between happy and safe while making the best use of public funds

It is divided into four sections:

The administrative section	The support section
Basic information about who the plan belongs to, who is involved in producing it.	Describes the support the person requires and what people who know and love the person believe is important for the person to be healthy and safe.
The person's section	**The action section**
This sections describes the 'positive reputation' of the person and lists and three prioritised lists of what the person sees as important to them.	This section checks reality against the plan and, if something is important to the person and is not present, an action is set to change this.

---

[11] Source: www.elpnet.com

PATH (Planning Alternative Tomorrows with Hope) [12]

PATH was developed by Jack Pearpoint, Marsha Forest and John O'Brien from 1991 onwards.

> *"PATH is there when a situation is complex and will require concerted action, engaging other people and resources, over a longish period in order to make an important vision real."*

Step 1 - "the dream"
The facilitator asks the service user his/her personal vision of the future, it can be general or specific. Someone can draw graphics of what is being said or described at this time for visual recollection later on. Other people can comment and be included, but this must be agreed by the service user first. The dream guides and gives direction to the rest of the meeting.

Step 2 - sensing the goal
This step requires all participants to imagine that they are one year ahead but back at the meeting with the same people, same place. The facilitator will ask them to describe how they have got to that point and how it feels to be living in a better future. There are two rules to this stage, all goals recorded have to be both positive and possible.

Step 3 - now
Step 3 examines the situation now and analyses the tension between where the group is now and where they want to be in a year's time. It is this tension that gives energy and diversity to the process.

Step 4 - enrol/who's on board?
No one person will be able to achieve all of the goals singlehandedly, this step identifies who is needed to be contacted for support, as well as naming the people who may be standing in the way of progression so that they can be contacted and persuaded otherwise.

Step 5 - how are we going to build strength?
This can sometimes be a very important step in identifying what the group will need to do in order to maintain strength and commitment to the goals. It can sometimes be as simple as meeting regularly or supporting each other by phone. Sometimes it means acknowledging and changing destructive patterns in the group.

Step 6 - three/six month goals
The facilitator will ask the group to set a date for the next meeting as well as setting possible smaller meetings to check progress in-between times.

Step 7 - first steps
First steps are identified and the date for another meeting set.

---

[12] Source: *PATH: A workbook for planning positive, possible futures* (1993) Pearpoint, O'Brien, Forest

MAPS (Making Action Plans)

MAPs is a planning style developed by Judith Snow, Jack Pearpoint and Marsha Forest with support from John O'Brien and others. It was used first as a tool for helping disabled children integrate into mainstream schools but is now used more widely in PERSON-CENTRED PLANNING with children and adults.

MAPs is typically used in a meeting lasting 2-3 hours with the person and those close to him or her. It can also be used one to one. If used in a meeting it is essential that there are two facilitators, one to guide the process and the second to record it in pictures/colours/symbols (graphically). The MAPs process has eight steps.

Step 1 – what is the MAP?

Used as a 'warm up' the facilitator will ask the group individually what they think a map is, different explanations can be given, such as 'helps people to find their way through unknown territory' or 'helps people see where they are now and where they need to go'.

Step 2 – what is their history?

Told by the service user and those who have known them for the longest amount of time, a lifeline can be used here. The story can often come as a shock for others present who have only ever dealt with the person in the present times and may help service providers to understand how the past experiences reflect the current behaviours.

Step 3 – what are their dreams?

Similar to PATH it can also be represented graphically. The service user can describe their dreams metaphorically, some may be specific, others more general, but they must come from them, no one else! This step is central to the MAP process.

Step 4 – what are their nightmares?

This can be a difficult subject for some, however, just as dreaming gives the group something to work towards, naming the nightmares gives the group something to work away from. It is useful in allowing the group and the individual to express their fears and have them acknowledged. It may become clear that the person is very close to their nightmare now or that the most likely service 'solution' such as putting them back in the institution would be a return to the nightmare.

Step 5 – who is the person?

The service user can use all kinds of descriptive words here to sum up who they are, what makes them tick, their personality and characteristics.

Step 6 – what are their gifts, strengths and talents?

This step reverses the usual process of focusing on the person's problems and instead looks for the positive things that can be built on in the action plan. The entire group can participate in this part of the process.

Step 7 - what does the person need to achieve the dream and avoid the nightmare?

In this step people start to think about the people and resources needed to help the person move towards the dream and away from the nightmare.

Step 8 - Action Plan

The Action Plan sets out specifically who will do what by when.

RELEVANT LEGISLATION SURROUNDING PCP

The following section is purely for reference and may give the reader greater insight into the rise and popularity of the PCP Approach. The Acts are listed in reverse date order.

VALUING PEOPLE – WHITE PAPER DEPARTMENT OF HEALTH 2001

"People with learning disabilities can lead full and rewarding lives as many already do. But others find themselves pushed to the margins of our society. And almost all encounter prejudice, bullying, insensitive treatment and discrimination at some time in their lives. Such prejudice and discrimination – no less hurtful for often being unintentional – has a very damaging impact. It leads to your world becoming smaller, opportunities more limited, a withdrawal from wider society so time is spent only with family, carers or other people with learning disabilities. What's also a real cause for concern and anxiety is that many parents of learning disabled children face difficulties in finding the right care, health services, education and leisure opportunities for their sons and daughters. At best, they can feel obstacles are constantly put in their way by society. At worst, they feel abandoned by the rest of us. We have to change this situation if we are to achieve our goal of a modern society in which everyone is valued and has the chance to play their full part. There has been progress – often through the efforts of families, voluntary organizations and people with learning disabilities themselves. But a great deal more needs to be done. This White Paper sets out this Government's commitment to improving the life chances of people with learning disabilities. It shows how we will meet this commitment by working closely with local councils, the health service, voluntary organizations and most importantly with people with learning disabilities and their families to provide new opportunities for those with learning disabilities to lead full and active lives. I know the publication of a White Paper, however good its proposals, does not itself solve problems. The challenge for us all is to deliver the vision set out in this document so the lives of many thousands of people with learning disabilities will be brighter and more fulfilling. It is a challenge I am determined this Government will meet." (Tony Blair – Foreword, Valuing People)

HEALTH AND SOCIAL CARE ACT 2012

This act forms an umbrella under which all vulnerable people in whatever care setting are protected. It replaces the previous CARE STANDARDS ACT 2000 which replaced the registered Homes Act 1984.

The Act follows the National Care Standards Commission (NCSC) which later became the Commission for social Care Inspection (CSCI) and now is the Care Quality Commission (CQC)

The government introduced National Minimum Standards and established the General Social Care Council (GSCC) for England and the Care Council for Wales. These work towards raising the standards of practice through codes of conduct and practice.

The Act requires that any agency supplying care to a person within their own home (domiciliary) must be registered.

EQUALITY ACT 2010

This act replaced most of the previous Disability Discrimination
Act 1995. Under this act, disabled people cannot be discriminated against in respect of:

- Employment
- Education
- Access to goods, facilities and services
- Buying or renting land or property

In April 2005 a new act was passed by parliament which amends or extends existing provisions in the DDA 1995 including;

- Making it unlawful for operators of transport vehicles to discriminate against disabled people
- Making it easier for disabled people to rent property and for tenants to make disability – related applications
- Making sure that private clubs with 25 or more members cannot keep disabled people out, just because they have a disability
- Extending protection to cover people who have HIV, cancer and multiple sclerosis from the moment it is diagnosed
- Ensuring that discrimination law covers all the activities of the public sector
- Requiring public bodies to promote equality of opportunity for disabled people

MENTAL CAPACITY ACT 2005

Within this act neglect was criminalized i.e. a person accused of neglecting another individual will have broken the law and can be dealt with within the criminal justice system. The act is underpinned by 5 key principles;

- An individual is assumed to be capable unless proven otherwise
- An individual should be supported to make their own decisions
- An individual has the right to make unorthodox decisions
- The individual's best interests must be the focus
- Any intervention should be as unrestrictive as possible

This act will help and offer guidance to people who can make some decisions about their treatment, and live a mainly independent life, but who may need help with some other aspects of their being – such as being able to live independently but needing help to cook hot meals.

This Act also incorporates 'advanced decisions' which is when someone with mental capacity decides that they do not want a particular type of treatment if they lack capacity in the future even a doctor must respect this decision.

This replaced the ENDURING POWER Of ATTORNEY ACT 1988

NATIONAL SERVICE FRAMEWORK FOR OLDER PEOPLE

A National Service Framework (NSF) for older people (aged over 55) was published by the Department of Health in 2001. It is a 10 year framework for improving the health and social care of older people in England. It looks at how best to diagnose, assess and treat people with dementia, as well as developing an integrated mental health service between local authorities and independent healthcare providers.

THE HUMAN RIGHTS ACT 1998

The Human Rights Act 1998 gives further legal effect in the UK to the fundamental rights and freedoms contained in the European Convention on Human Rights. These rights not only impact matters of life and death, they also affect the rights you have in your everyday life: what you can say and do, your beliefs, your right to a fair trial and other similar basic entitlements.

Most rights have limits to ensure that they do not unfairly damage other people's rights. However, certain rights such as the right not to be tortured can never be limited by a court or anybody else.
You have the responsibility to respect other people's rights, and they must respect yours. Your human rights are:

- the right to life
- freedom from torture and degrading treatment
- freedom from slavery and forced labour
- the right to liberty
- the right to a fair trial
- the right not to be punished for something that wasn't a crime when you did it
- the right to respect for private and family life
- freedom of thought, conscience and religion, and freedom to express your beliefs
- freedom of expression
- freedom of assembly and association
- the right to marry and to start a family
- the right not to be discriminated against in respect of these rights and freedoms
- the right to peaceful enjoyment of your property
- the right to an education
- the right to participate in free elections
- the right not to be subjected to the death penalty

If any of these rights and freedoms are breached, you have a right to an effective solution in law, even if the breach was by someone in authority, such as police officer.

DATA PROTECTION ACT 1998

This act governs the storage and processing of personal data held in manual records and on computers. Under this act, your rights are protected by forcing organizations to follow proper and sound practices, known as data protection principles (DPP).

The data protection Act contains 8 principles which state that all data must be;

1. Processed fairly and lawfully
2. Obtained and used only for specified and lawful purposes
3. Is adequate, relevant and not excessive
4. Accurate, and where necessary kept up to date
5. Kept for no longer than necessary
6. Processed in accordance with the individuals rights
7. Kept secure
8. Transferred only to countries that offer adequate data protection

HEALTH ACT 1999

This came into force in 2000 and aims to end the division between health services (funded and provided by the NHS) and social services (run by local councils). The difference between health and social care and which 'illnesses or 'situation' is covered by which agency is very confusing. Regularly hospital beds which are funded by 'health' are often blocked due to 'social' not being ready with a care package for them. Ultimately this kind of treatment lacks quality.

NHS AND COMMUNITY CARE ACT 1990

Requires social services to assess an individual's needs for living within the community. They should also provide clear procedures for complaints, comments, and registration and inspection requirements. Reviews of a person's ability to contribute should also be taken into consideration.

THE MENTAL HEALTH ACT 1983

Many people receive specialist mental health care and treatment in the community. However, some people can experience severe mental health problems that require admission to hospital for assessment and treatment. People can only be detained if the strict criteria laid down in the Act are met. The person must be suffering from a mental disorder as defined by the Act. An application for assessment or treatment must be supported in writing by two registered medical practitioners. The recommendation must include a statement about why an assessment and/or treatment is necessary, and why other methods of dealing with the patient are not appropriate.

THE HEALTH AND SAFETY ACT 1974

Requires the employer and the employee to take responsibility for health and safety whilst carrying out work. The act requires employers to provide a safe working environment and supply any equipment required to carry out the role i.e. PPE. This act safeguards the person with dementia by ensuring they are not put at risk of harm whilst using the service.

PROMINENT FIGURES IN WORLD OF RESEARCH INTO PCP

There are several key figures within this field, and they have produced many articles and studies that you may like to read. They will enhance your knowledge of how, why and when, the practices we carry out today began and where they are headed.

- **Helen Sanderson** Heads HSA (Helen Sanderson Associates) and is also the expert advisor in person centred approaches to the Valuing People Support Team.
- **Peter Kinsella** is the Managing Director of Paradigm, which he founded in 1999. He has consulted widely across the UK, Europe, USA and Australia on issues including supported living, individual budgets, self directed support, commissioning, service evaluation, service provision, funding, leadership and organisational development.
- **Simon Duffy** is the Chief Executive of 'In Control'. Simon guides In Control's strategy and the coherence of its philosophy and practice. His main focus is on developing In Control's role as a Network of Social Innovation and thinking about the impact of self-direction in health and education, how to promote community and citizenship development and the future policy framework for Social Care. Simon is also working on a book on the wider reform of the welfare state to promote citizenship
- **Michael W Smull** is a disability rights advocate -*"The continuing gap between best and typical practice in supporting people with disabilities is disturbing. It has been more than a decade since we learned how to do plans with people that reflected how they wanted to live rather than what was wrong with them."* (September 2000)
- **John O'Brien and Connie Lyle O'Brien** researched and found any group of people if asked what makes life worth living and what makes for a good life, tend to say the same things. John O'Brien outlined the' five service accomplishments' or the 'five dimensions of inclusion'.

The above list is not exhaustive and in no way undermines the contribution of other people who have had input into this field.

LEARN CARE EXCEL

Matthews House
21 Thorley Park Road
Bishops Stortford
CM23 3NG

Tel: 07774 880880

info@learncareexcel.co.uk
www.learncareexcel.co.uk

Printed in Great Britain
by Amazon

28739898R00020